IMAGES
of America

CAHOKIA

Cover Photograph: This picture is dated August 14, 1921. The children are posing on early-model automobiles at an unidentified Cahokia farm. (Courtesy Marguerite Mischke.)

IMAGES
of America

CAHOKIA

Denita Reed

ARCADIA
PUBLISHING

Published by Arcadia Publishing
Charleston, South Carolina

Library of Congress Catalog Card Number: 98-87145

For all general information contact Arcadia Publishing at:
Telephone 843-853-2070
Fax 843-853-0044
E-mail sales@arcadiapublishing.com
For customer service and orders:
Toll-Free 1-888-313-2665

Visit us on the Internet at www.arcadiapublishing.com

*This book is sincerely dedicated
to all the former, current, and future residents of Cahokia.
The Cahokia community celebrates its rich history and heritage
through its people and their achievements.
The people are the community and the history.*

CONTENTS

ACKNOWLEDGMENTS

I would like to sincerely thank all the many individuals and institutions who have allowed me to use their special photos in this book. The courtesy credits listed on each photo identify the lender of the image. I applaud each and every one of you for your generosity and willingness to share your memories. I especially enjoyed hearing your many stories and will carry them and pass them along as I am able. Special thanks to Holy Family Parish, who opened their treasured archives with unlimited access, and to the Cahokia Public Library District for their sponsorship of *Historic Moments*, which provided community members with a location to bring their photos. I am equally grateful to Todd Eschman of *The Herald*, Jason White and Mike Viola of the *Cahokia-Dupo Journal*, and Susan Luberda of the *St. Louis Post-Dispatch* for wonderful publicity which helped me reach community members. I especially wish to thank my boss, M. Loretta Lopinot, Director of the Cahokia Public Library District, and my son, John Nicholas Reed, for their assistance in entering the text of this publication into the word processor and for their editing suggestions. A very special thank-you to my husband, John Robert Reed, who lent tremendous support to this project and who continues to give unselfishly of his time and talent to the community in his leadership role as Chairperson of the Holy Family Tricentennial.

INTRODUCTION

The historic village of Cahokia was established in 1699 as a mission among the Tamaroa and Cahokia Indians. The name "Cahokia" is derived from the Native-American word meaning "wild geese." It is the oldest permanent Euro-American settlement in the Mississippi River Valley.

Priests from Quebec founded the Illinois mission some 65 years before the founding of its nearest major city, St. Louis. Though linked closely to the city of St. Louis and the Metro-East area, Cahokia has retained its own unique character based on its distinctive French heritage.

Cahokia is located in the rich, fertile region known as the American Bottoms, a low tract of land extending from Alton to Chester. Floods have plagued the community from the early 1800s to 1957, the most destructive of which were recorded in 1844, 1892, and 1903. Despite the difficulties caused by the floods, the people of Cahokia have persevered and the population has continued to grow throughout its history.

In 1700, there were reportedly 30 white fur traders among the local Native-American tribes. In 1752, the population of 136 listed mostly fur traders and farmers, but also included African-American and Native-American slaves. By 1776, the population had grown to 3,000. In the village there were two distinct communities, the French and the Native American. The races mingled in trade and worship and sometimes intermarried.

The history of the Cahokia community tells the story of an expanding nation. The French were the first to open this region to discovery and exploration. The names of the great explorers and pioneers who showed wisdom and courage as they attempted to explore the vast wilderness empire, including Father Marquette, Joliet, LaSalle, Father St. Cosme, and Father Gibault, are well remembered in the community.

After France's defeat in the French and Indian War, Cahokia came under British rule in 1763. Villagers remained loyal to the French, however, until 1778, when George Rogers Clark peacefully took Cahokia for the Americans during the Revolutionary War. Fort Bowman, which was established within the village boundaries, became the westernmost American fort during the Revolution.

The community experienced its greatest increase in population during the years of 1950–58, when the populace increased to 15,000. The vast rise in Cahokia's population at this time can be attributed to Oliver Parks, a real estate developer who responded to the need for low-cost housing for young couples after World War II by developing subdivisions of prefabricated homes in the community. Young couples were eager to move to this thriving community, which offered new, inexpensive homes, spacious yards, and good schools.

In recalling our history as we prepare for our community's 300th year in 1999, we remember and respect the great events which shaped our community. We honor the courageous pioneers and noble leaders who devoted their lives for the good of the all. But we also pay homage to those individuals to whom there is no memorial or recorded history, remembering all the unnamed men and women whose good deeds and exemplary daily duties helped the community to survive and flourish.

It is not always the great events which are important in the life of a community. It is the people who truly shape the community. The example of church and community leaders, the daily education and care of children, the routine life of community members, the celebrations of special occasions . . . these are the real events. These are the events that this pictorial history of Cahokia focuses on—our churches, our schools, our weddings, our children, our families, our community, and our celebrations.

As Cahokia prepares for its 300th anniversary celebration in 1999, may we be strengthened as a community as we preserve our heritage and anticipate our future.

One

Our Churches

In 1699, Holy Family Church was the community and the community was the church. Our churches continue to be the foundation for the community today.

Dedicated in 1799, the historic church of the Holy Family is the finest example of French colonial architecture in the United States. The simplicity of the building gives it a majestic elegance. In 1913, the church was covered with white clapboard siding to protect it. The original chapel of the Holy Family Mission, dating from 1699, was destroyed by fire. Even after the settlement of Cahokia expanded into a thriving colonial village, the church, following French custom, served as its focal point. (Courtesy Holy Family Parish.)

This picture shows the interior of the Log Church, c. 1914. The occasion was an open meeting of the Western Catholic Union, Branch 161. Principal speaker Hon. William Heckenkamp of Quincy, IL, supreme president of the society, sits at head of the central

table. Father Hynes, pastor of Holy Family, sits at his left. Father Pete Engle of St. Elizabeth's Parish is pictured at his right. (Courtesy Holy Family Parish.)

Holy Family Rock Church, completed and dedicated in 1892, is shown here during the flood of the same year. The photo was taken on May 23. (Courtesy Holy Family Parish.)

Reverend Joseph Henry Mueller was appointed to take charge of the Parish of the Holy Family in Cahokia on October 10, 1928. Born in Pittsburgh, Pennsylvania, he revered the historic Log Church and was instrumental in rescuing it from destruction. He served the parish until 1971. (Courtesy Holy Family Parish.)

This photo shows the rear view of Holy Family Log Church, Holy Family Rock Church, and the cemetery. The cemetery at Holy Family dates from the origin of the parish in 1699 and is the earliest burial ground of settlers in the Midwest. (Courtesy Cahokia Courthouse State Historic Site and James C. Hammond, Photographer.)

Florence and Rose Jerome pose for a First Communion portrait, c. 1910. (Courtesy John Reed.)

This Holy Family First Communion class picture is dated May 12, 1916. Nelia Hartman and Jeanette Hartman are identified as the first and second girls on the second row. Pastor John F. Weimar was the pastor of Holy Family in 1916. (Courtesy Rita LePere Howell.)

This First Communion class photo was taken outside of Holy Family Rock Church on Holy Thursday, April 10, 1928. (Courtesy Family of Sonny and June Levin.)

A Confirmation class proudly poses with Holy Family's Father Joseph Mueller outside the Holy Family Rock Church side entrance in 1936. Identified are Aurelia Schmitt (second row, fourth student from the left) and Sonny Levin (third row, seventh student from the left). (Courtesy Family of Sonny and June Levin.)

Father Joseph Mueller and Holy Family Parish altar boys pose for a group portrait in the early 1940s. Mearl Justus is pictured in the back row, third from the left. This photo also depicts the beautiful altar and painted walls of the Rock Church interior. (Courtesy St. Clair County Sheriff Mearl Justus.)

The Holy Family School Primary Building was dedicated in 1945. The altar boy at the far left is Herman O'Guinn; the candle bearer is Bernard Reed; Father Joseph Mueller is in front of the cross; and Mearl Justus is pictured at far right. Bishop Henry Althoff presides. (Courtesy St. Clair County Sheriff Mearl Justus.)

The Holy Family Graduation Class of 1945 is pictured here in front of the Jarrot Mansion. From left to right they are as follows: (front row) Jeannie Erndle and Ron Sauget; (middle row) Sister Ursula, Jeanette Gischer, Marlene Touchette, Doris Jerome, Victoria Huetsch, Margaret Hoffman, and Father Joseph Mueller; (back row) Vincent Michael, James O'Guinn, Mearl Justus, and Leo Dooley. (Courtesy St. Clair County Sheriff Mearl Justus.)

Sister Anna Linda poses with First Communicants Janet Schuh (back to camera) and Kathy Drexler in 1957. Holy Family Rock Church appears in the background. (Courtesy Eleanor Schuh.)

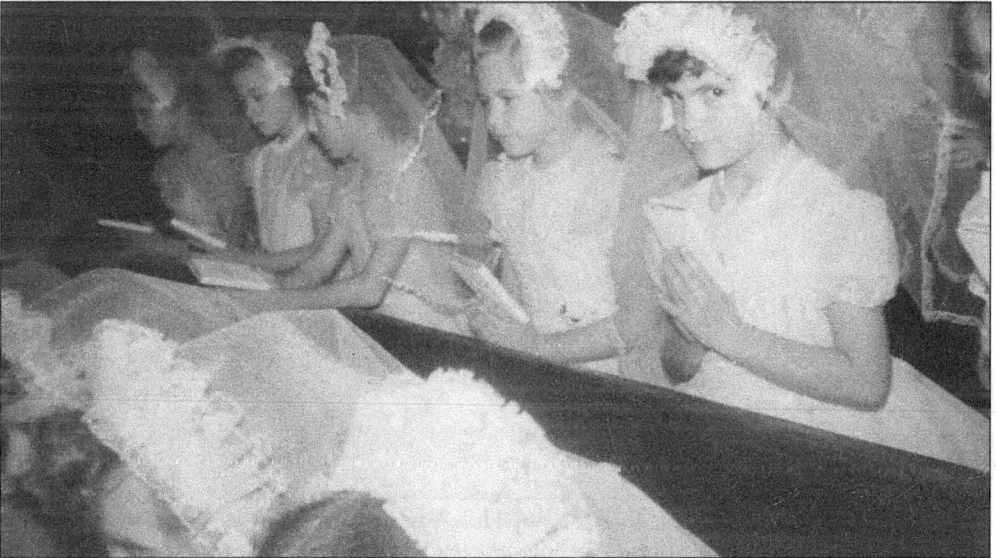

The author fondly recalls her own First Communion Day in 1961 at Holy Family Church. I was a second-grader named Denita Santagato. (Courtesy Denita Reed.)

The memorable date 1776 is stamped on the parish bell of Holy Family Church. The bell is believed to have been brought to Cahokia by traders from the east. The fact that Cahokia was the westernmost bastion in the Revolutionary War makes the inscribed date especially significant. (Courtesy Holy Family Parish; credit Peter Ferman.)

These revered religious articles, cherished by Holy Family Parish, are believed to have been brought by the earliest missionaries—a candlestick, exquisitely designed in old world handiwork; a missal, printed in Antwerp in 1668; a ciborium, made of silver and plated with gold; and a monstrance, made of brass and decorated with fancy diemarks. (Courtesy Holy Family Parish.)

The interior of Holy Family Log Church is shown in this photo. Heavy black walnut timbers, 12 inches wide, 6 inches thick, and 14 feet high, formed the walls. Spaced about 1 foot apart, they are mortised into extra heavy timber sills set on a stone foundation. The church was officially dedicated as a National Historic Landmark on April 25, 1971. (Courtesy E.B. Hardwig.)

The Mission Cross commemorating events held at Holy Family Parish in 1864 and 1897 proclaims, "He who perseveres to the end shall be saved." (Courtesy Cahokia Unit School District #187 teacher Sue Henderson.)

In 1997, parishioner Andy Eftink handcrafted this wooden cross for the front of the new Holy Family Church. The cross is a visible symbol of the parish's preparation for the tricentennial (1999) and the Catholic Church Jubilee Celebration (2000). It was made to complement the old Mission Cross in the Log Church. (Courtesy Cahokia Unit School District #187 teacher Sue Henderson.)

Reverend John T. Myler, current pastor of Holy Family Parish, has been instrumental in planning for the 300th anniversary of the parish. (Courtesy Herald Editor Todd Eschman.)

Mt. Calvary Lutheran Church holds the distinction of being the first Protestant Church dedicated in Cahokia in 1929. The first Confirmation class of 1931, pictured here with Pastor Fleer, consisted of, from left to right, LaVerne Levin, Jack Gilbert, Alice Pulcher, Melvin Julien, Dorothy Levin, and Louis Levin. (Courtesy Mt. Calvary Lutheran Church.)

The Mt. Calvary Lutheran Church Confirmation class of 1936 consisted of the following, from left to right: (first row) Reverend Edward Fleer and Elmer Levin; (second row) Louise Levin, Mary Jane Svoboda, and Lucille Portell. (Courtesy Mt. Calvary Lutheran Church.)

The Mt. Calvary Lutheran Church Confirmation class of 1938 was comprised of the following, from left to right: (front row) Ella Mae Pulcher, Elnora Levin, Edith Osborne, Delores Pluff, and Carlene Portell; (back row) Howard Chattillion, Edgar Levin, Edward Levin, Edward Svoboda, and Pastor Fleer. (Courtesy Mt. Calvary Lutheran Church.)

Mt. Calvary Lutheran Church's first church site belongs to the Apostolic Pentecostal Church today. The old millstones on the right were placed on the property by the Chattillion family as a permanent memorial during the Cahokia 250th anniversary celebration in 1949. The stones were found on the Chattillion farm adjoining Route 3 at the Prairie du Pont Channel bridge. (Courtesy Holy Family Parish.)

The ground-breaking ceremony for Mt. Calvary Lutheran Church was held on October 5, 1958. The building committee members shown here are, from left to right, John Pogue, Fred Bodendieck, Eugene Pulcher, Reverend Don C. Preisinger, and Paul Longenbaugh. (Courtesy Mt. Calvary Lutheran Church.)

Mt. Calvary Lutheran Church organist William Osborne performs here on Easter Sunday, 1998. The organ was regarded as one of the finest in the state when it was purchased and dedicated on May 22, 1949. It is a 16-rank, two-manual, Moller pipe organ. (Courtesy Mt. Calvary Lutheran Church and Jane Osborne.)

Leanore Pluff, charter member of Mt. Calvary Lutheran Church, was born September 4, 1900. She resides in Cahokia today. (Courtesy Mt. Calvary Lutheran Church.)

The Cahokia Park United Methodist Church traces its history back to 1894. The church bulletin from 1916 listed the congregation as "The Friendly Church." Members are pictured here at a celebration meal following the last service on January 29, 1947, at the Bond Avenue Methodist Episcopal Church, located at Tenth and Bond, East St. Louis, Illinois. (Courtesy Cahokia Park United Methodist Church.)

Bond Avenue Methodist Episcopal Church members voted to relocate to this Mildred Avenue location in Cahokia. The cornerstone was laid for the sanctuary in 1947. The first service was held in May 1948. (Courtesy Cahokia Park United Methodist Church.)

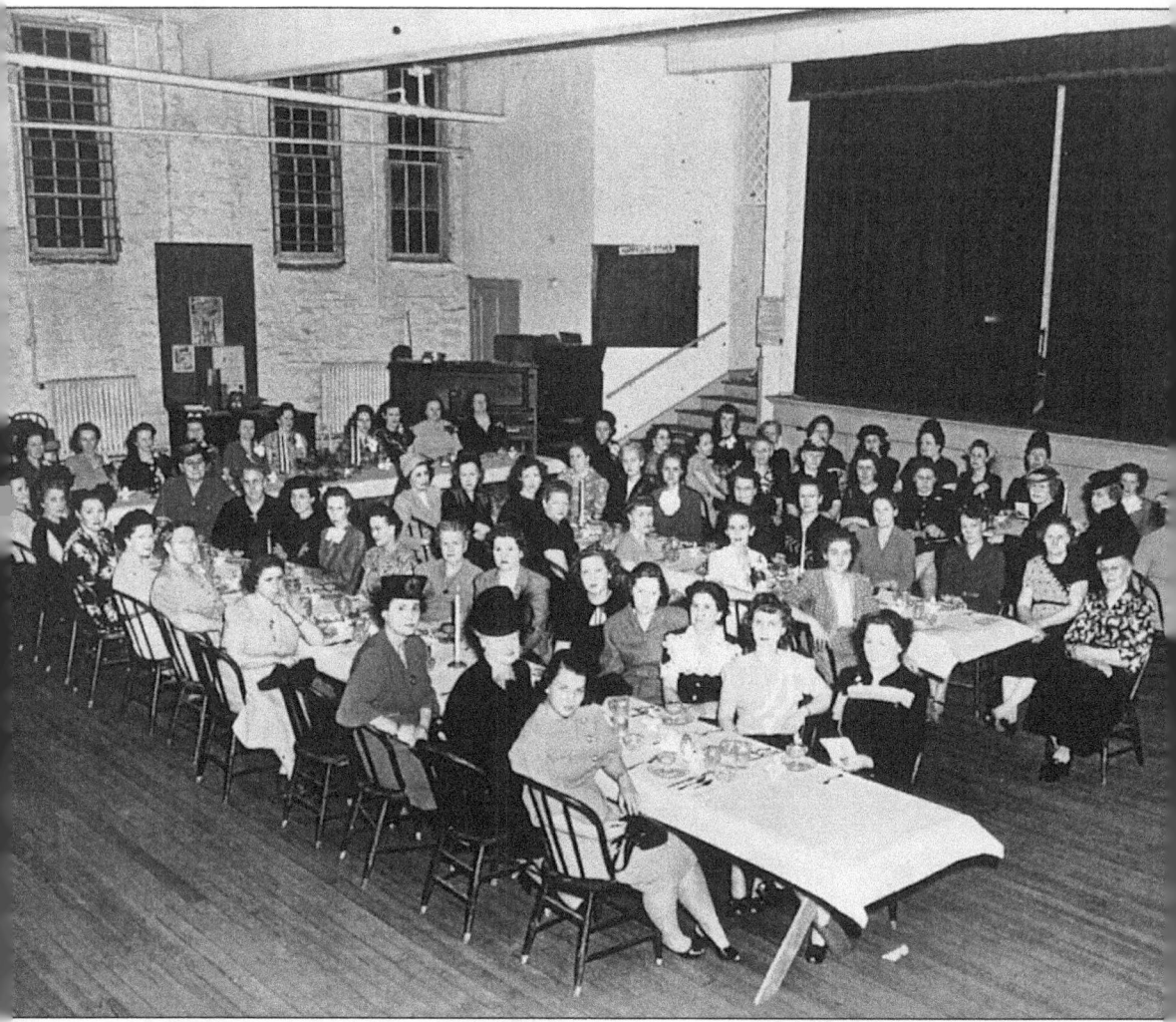

Mrs. Enid Densmore organized the Kappa Delta Sunday school class in 1922 for the Bond Avenue Methodist Episcopal Church. This 25th anniversary celebration of the Kappa Delta class was held on February 11, 1947, at St. Paul's Methodist Episcopal Church. (Courtesy Cahokia Park United Methodist Church.)

Fire destroyed the Cahokia Park United Methodist Church on July 20, 1987. Church services were held at Emeth Lodge #1030 in Cahokia during the rebuilding. (Courtesy Gail Callahan.)

Cahokia Park United Methodist Church was rebuilt with the same basic building plan and an added education wing. The congregation returned to their sanctuary on July 17, 1988. A Service of Consecration and Open House was held October 2, 1988. Today, the congregation continues to offer the love of Christ to the community, to provide opportunities for missions, and to discipline people of all ages in the Christian faith. (Courtesy Eva and Homer Adele.)

The congregation of Cahokia Park United Methodist Church celebrated 100 years of ministry on June 1, 1997. Shown here are the following, from left to right: (front row) Reverend John Turner (served 1954–1958), Reverend R. James Weiss (served 1952–1954), Reverend Dowain McKiou (served 1957–1964), and Reverend John Annable (served 1978–1988); (back row) Reverend James Schuetz (served 1988–1994), Reverend Tim Ozment (1994–present), Dr. C. Calvin Ryan (served 1947–1948), and Reverend Dan Harry (served as associate 1982–1984). (Courtesy Cahokia Park United Methodist Church.)

As the population of Cahokia continued to grow, the Catholic Parish of the Holy Family welcomed its sister parish of St. Catherine Laboure to minister to Catholics. Father John Walsh, pastor of the newly formed parish, is pictured at the ground-breaking ceremony in May 1961. (Courtesy Eleanor Schuh.)

St. Catherine Laboure parishioner Tom Schuh attends the ground-breaking ceremony. The site for the new parish is located at the corner of Jerome and Rome.(Courtesy Eleanor Schuh.)

Reverend Herbert M. Schafale, a minister of the Evangelical and Reformed Church, was appointed to establish a new church in the Cahokia-Centreville area. The first worship service was held on September 13, 1959, at this temporary location on Mildred Avenue. One hundred and forty-five people attended. (Courtesy Bethel United Church of Christ.)

The ground-breaking ceremony for Bethel Evangelical and Reformed Church, located at 2200 Camp Jackson, was held on July 8, 1962. Reverend Henry J. Damm, board of National Missions, and Reverend Herbert M. Schafale, pastor, are pictured here. Mrs. Louise Roland, the oldest member of the congregation, turned the first spade of soil. (Courtesy Bethel United Church of Christ.)

Bethel Evangelical and Reformed Church (United Church of Christ) held its first services at the new $76,000 church on Sunday, July 7, 1963. The congregation of 240 members moved into the new structure from temporary quarters on Mildred Avenue. This first unit of a three-step plan would include a fellowship hall, sanctuary, and Christian education unit. (Courtesy Bethel United Church of Christ.)

Reverend Herbert M. Schafale, the first pastor of Bethel Evangelical and Reformed Church of the United Church of Christ, poses with the Confirmation class of May 3, 1964. (Courtesy Bethel United Church of Christ.)

Reverend Ann Asper Wilson served Bethel during the years of 1974–81. She had the distinction of being the first female minister in the Metro-East area. (Courtesy Elna and Graham Rosenberger.)

Two

OUR SCHOOLS

Our schools are the institutions where young people are shaped and molded on their journey to adulthood. God Bless all past, present, and future educators.

By 1836, Reverend Peter Doutreluingue, pastor of Holy Family Mission Church, had secured a building in the center of the village near the church for a convent and school. Mother Febronie Fontbonne, the Superior of the Cahokia Mission, was a native of Valbenoite, France, and 26 years of age when she arrived in Cahokia. (Courtesy Archives of the Sisters of St. Joseph of Carondelet, St. Louis Province.)

Sister St. Protais Deboille was ready with all the enthusiasm of her 21 years to devote the rest of her life to converting Native Americans. She fell ill in 1831 and had to leave St. Joseph's Institute, the name given by the sisters to the convent and school. Villagers lovingly referred to the school as "The Abbey." (Courtesy Archives of the Sisters of St. Joseph of Carondelet, St. Louis Province.)

The three Sisters of Saint Joseph who arrived on April 7, 1836, were welcomed as "angels from heaven" by Father Doutreluingue and the simple, pious villagers. The sisters made many friends among the kind-hearted Cahokians, who contributed in numerous ways to their comfort, besides warmly supporting the school. Pictured here is Sister Febronie Chapellon. (Courtesy Archives of the Sisters of St. Joseph of Carondelet, St. Louis Province.)

Adorers of the Most Precious Blood was the religious order assigned to Holy Family School and Parish in 1889. They served the people faithfully for 100 years. Two members of the order are pictured here with a school class from the late 1920s. Sonny Levin is the fifth boy from the left in the front row. (Courtesy Family of Sonny and June Levin.)

Sister Mary Yvonne is pictured with her Holy Family School class of grades one, two, three, and four. This photo was taken February 3, 1931, in the converted Jarrot Mansion Ballroom classroom. The Mission of the Holy Family Parish used the Jarrot Mansion as a schoolhouse from 1905 to 1941. (Courtesy Family of Sonny and June Levin.)

This June 1941 photograph was probably one of the last taken while the Jarrot Mansion Ballroom served as a classroom. (Courtesy Cahokia Courthouse State Historic Site.)

The Holy Family School class photo in 1934 was taken in front of the Jarrot Mansion Schoolhouse. Reverend Joseph H. Mueller is pictured at right. Pete Montine is the sixth student in the second row. (Courtesy Montine Family.)

The Holy Family Class of 1938 graduation photo was taken in front of Holy Family Rock Church. (Courtesy Cahokia Courthouse State Historic Site.)

In 1937, the Holy Family School second-grade class was photographed in front of Holy Family Rock Church. (Courtesy Montine Family.)

Holy Family School fourth-graders pose in front of the parish rectory in 1941. The students are pictured, from left to right, as follows: (front row) Laverne Hoock, Jim Jerome, Albert Schmitz, Vincent Michael, Mearl Justus, Bernard Reid, Mike Koch, Jerry Callahan, and George Bitzenberger; (back row) three unidentified students, Marlene Touchette, Jeanette Gischer, Leo Dooley, James O'Guinn, Doris Jerome, Vickie Huetsch, Doris Smith, Margie Hoffman, and Sister Mary Vita. (Courtesy Jerry Callahan.)

This photograph from 1942 is Holy Family School's seventh-grade class. Sister Eileen is the Precious Blood Sister at right. Bo Jerome is the seventh student from the left in the first row. Norma Rey is the twelfth student from the left in the second row. Jeanette Jerome is on Norma's right. Donald Justus is in the third row, in a striped shirt. (Courtesy Montine Family.)

Sister Mary Vita is pictured here in front of Holy Family Rock Church with her Holy Family third-grade class, c. 1940. Jerry Callahan (top row, far left) and Albert E. Viner (top row, fifth boy from the left) have been identified. (Courtesy Jerry Callahan.)

This Jerome Elementary School class photo is from 1894. An early school register, located at current Cahokia Unit School District #187 Board Building, lists some of the following surnames: Adele, Etienne, Jacquot, Lopinot, Nadeaux, Pluff, and Sauget. Identified in this picture are August "Gus" Adele (back row, fourth from the left) and Maria Adele Sauget (back row, sixth from the left). (Courtesy Homer Adele.)

In 1894, Cahokia School was located at Second and Main and housed grades one through eight. Identified in this picture are Eugene Sauget (fourth student from the left in the top row) and Leo Sauget (first student from the left in the first row). Leo Sauget served as mayor of Sauget, formerly Monsanto, from 1926 to 1969. (Courtesy Georgette Sauget.)

This class photo is from Cahokia School in 1918–19. The students pictured here are, from left to right, as follows: (front row) Ernest Sauget, Archie Palmier, Theophile Sauget, ? Schaefer, and Wallace Sauget; (second row) Lottie Palmier, Joseph Lucher, Walter Lucher, Mary Lucher, Ervin Sauget, Carl Sauget, Beatrice Crabtree, and Ernest Sauget; (back row) Sophia Sauget, Lorraine Sauget, Clarence Sauget, Corrine Sauget, Robert Lucher, and Julia Schlemmer (teacher). (Courtesy Georgette Sauget and Mary Lucher Maness.)

Many of the same students, Saugets and Luchers, can be identified in this class photo of the Cahokia School from the same school year. (Courtesy Georgette Sauget.)

The entire school body of Cahokia School is pictured in this photo from 1921. Many students have memories of the fragrant honey-locust tree directly to the right of the building. (Courtesy Georgette Sauget.)

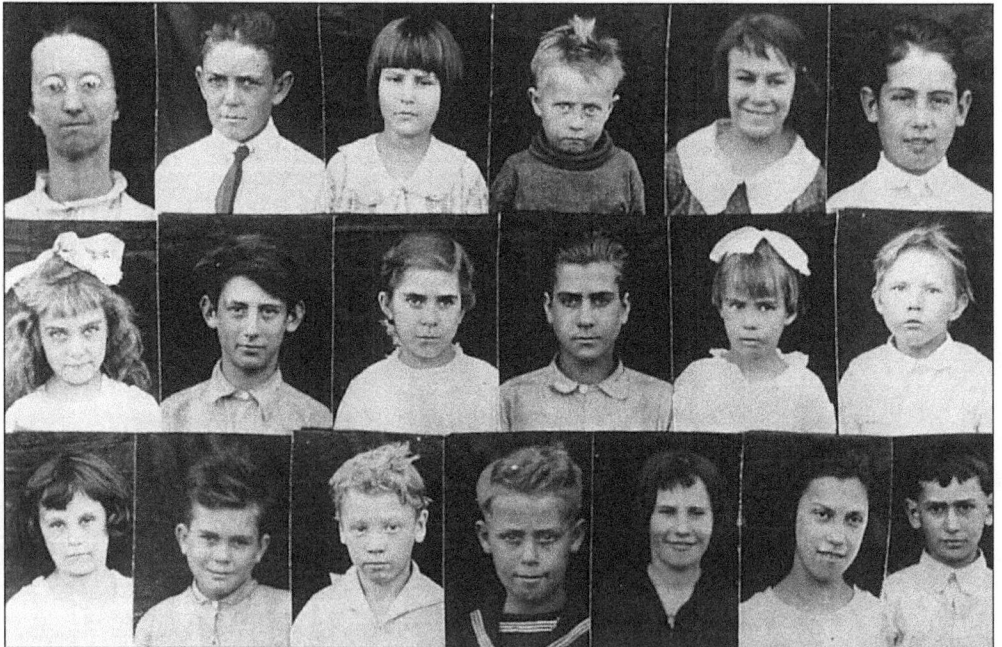

These individual photos were placed together to make a memorable composite of a Cahokia School class and their teacher. The picture is dated 1923. (Courtesy Georgette Sauget.)

The Cahokia School class of 1925 is pictured with their teacher, Mrs. Duckett (in the back row, center). Identified are Georgette Sauget (second row, fifth student from the left) and Charles White (first row, fifth student from the left). (Courtesy Georgette Sauget.)

Maplewood School students are pictured here in 1928. They are, from left to right, as follows: (front row) Clifford Vogt, Gary Hoock, and two unidentified students; (middle row) Rita DeMange and Mary Jane Svoboda; (back row) Merle Reed, Melvin Julien, Nicholas Adele, Ervin Vogt, and Miss Josephine Compton, teacher. (Courtesy John Reed.)

This photo, clearly marked "Cahokia School District #50," is believed to have been taken at Jerome School on September 14, 1931. (Courtesy Earl Chambers.)

This photo shows the interior of Jerome School in 1932. Mrs. Josephine Compton was the teacher. In this photograph are, from left to right, as follows: (front row) unidentified, Donald Osborne, unidentified, and Russell Jerome; (middle row) Marie Bennett, Edgar Levin, June Jerome, Homer Adele, unidentified, and Edward Levin; (in the row by the door) Gary Hoock, unidentified, unidentified, and Elmer Levin. (Courtesy Homer Adele.)

In this photo of the interior of Maplewood School, dated 1933, teacher Wendall Hoover stands by the blackboard. Student names listed on back of the photo included Wanda Downing, Lois Lane, Wilma Gray, Delmar Yates, Archie Smith, Opal Firestine, Helen Demetrulias, Mary Jane Svoboda, Russell McCoy, Mildred McCauley, LaVerne Levin, Cliff Latta, Gene Cunningham, and Melvin Julien. (Courtesy LaVerne Levin Cobb.)

Maplewood School's seventh-grade class with their teacher, Miss Perry, is pictured here in 1946–47. Phyllis Jerome has been identified as the first student in the bottom row. (Courtesy Phyllis Jerome Taylor.)

This Maplewood School class photo is dated 1939. (Courtesy Father Albert Jerome.)

This is Maplewood School's second-grade class with their teacher, Mrs. Miller, in 1947–1948. Among the students shown here are Jerry Groves (row three, sixth from the left), Janet Faskall (row two, third from the left), and Janet Herderhorst (row four, third from the left). (Courtesy Phyllis Jerome Taylor.)

The first orchestra of Cahokia, from Maplewood School, was organized in 1934. Mr. Hoover was the teacher, and Mr. Ed Wirth was the band director. (Courtesy LaVerne Levin Cobb.)

Cahokia High School students stand in front of the high school in 1961. The ultra-modern, 42-room, two-story brick building was dedicated on August 17, 1952. It cost $3,090,000 to build and $250,000 to furnish. The man kneeling has been identified as Fred McBride. Pictured standing are Bill Sims, unidentified, Glen Dick, David Levin, Pat Bland, Jerry Rachell, Lawrence Sanderson, and two unidentified individuals. (Courtesy Guy R. Baney.)

Charles Lindbergh, Oliver Lafayette Parks, and Boots Dempsey inspect the construction of the Parks aircraft factory/administration building in 1929. Parks, a pioneer aviation educator, founded Parks Air College on August 1, 1927, in a rented hanger at Lambert Field. He moved the school to Cahokia in the spring of 1928. (Courtesy Parks College Archives of Saint Louis University.)

This aerial view of Parks College campus was taken on September 1928. Note the tracks of the Columbia-Waterloo Railway. (Courtesy Parks College Archives of Saint Louis University.)

Feb 1929.

This aerial view of Parks Air College was taken on February 1929. In the early years, many pilots from across the United States came to visit and inspect the amazing new school. All became staunch supporters of the college. (Courtesy Parks College Archives of Saint Louis University.)

Rex, a 1928 Parks student, is pictured in a Cahokia yard during the founding year of the school. Students enjoyed the small-town atmosphere of the Cahokia location. (Courtesy Rita LePere Howell.)

Fighter cadets pose for a photo in front of the main hangar for Parks's flight training school in the 1940s. Parks Air College trained one-tenth of all Army Air Corps pilots who served in World War II. (Courtesy Parks College Archives of Saint Louis University.)

This photo of Parks Chapel was taken in May 1997. The building was originally constructed in 1941 as the first Parks library building, but was converted into a chapel in 1946 with the donation of the 113-acre campus to Saint Louis University by Oliver L. Parks. The steeple that was added in 1983 is a scale replica of the steeple on the Old Cathedral of St. Louis. (Courtesy Dolores Seats.)

Cahokia Unit School District #187 staff members Ed Wolf (principal of Wirth Middle School) and Cecilia Miller (teacher) display one of the classroom doors decorated by the students during the 1997 Christmas holidays. (Courtesy Denita Reed.)

Belleville Area College employees Ann Clayton and Francine Lafferty invite residents to participate in the school's Adult Continuing Education program. The college sponsors classes at various locations throughout the community for lifelong educational opportunities. (Courtesy Denita Reed.)

Three

OUR WEDDINGS

Weddings are occasions that are truly the most joyful of all of our celebrations.

Leo and Louise Sauget are pictured at their January 26, 1910 wedding. Attendants were Prosper Sauget and Amelia Palmier. Leo Sauget served the community of Monsanto as mayor from 1926 to 1969. Mayor Sauget was renowned for his remarkable devotion to the political arena during his long term. Mrs. Sauget was equally admired and respected for her commitment to families, social events, and charitable causes. (Courtesy Richard Sauget.)

Mr. and Mrs. Pluff request your presence at the marriage of their daughter, Elizabeth to A. L. Jerome, Monday, Nov. 25th, 1895, at 10 o'clock a.m., at the Holy Family Church, Cahokia, Ill.

This printed invitation announced the wedding of Elizabeth Pluff and Albert L. Jerome on November 25, 1895. The wedding took place at 10 a.m. at Holy Family Church. (Courtesy Father Albert Jerome.)

This is the wedding portrait of Elizabeth and Albert Jerome. (Courtesy Father Albert Jerome.)

The marriage of Fred and Clara
Pluff took place in November 1909.
(Courtesy Marion and Leon Pluff.)

Alfonce and Belle Levin were
married in 1910 in Cahokia.
(Courtesy LaVerne Levin Cobb.)

Arthur and Nelia LePere were married at Holy Family Church on May 3, 1910. (Courtesy Rita LePere Howell.)

Leo Walter Jerome and Matilda "Tillie" Kohler were wed on June 11, 1924. (Courtesy Father Albert Jerome.)

The wedding of Petronella "Pet" LePere and Butch Touchette took place at Holy Family Rock Church in 1930. Nine-year-old Rita LePere was the flower girl. Attendants in the back row were Eleanor Hartman, Pete LePere, Julius Touchette, and Clementine Montine. The wedding mass is reported to have been the first performed in Holy Family Rock Church by Father Joseph Mueller. (Courtesy Rita LePere Howell.)

Rita LePere typified the height of fashion in this photo dated 1936. She wore a beautiful cerise gown with a wine velvet cape as a bridesmaid at cousin Clementine Montine's wedding. Rita's career as a fashion buyer for Stix Baer & Fuller led her on many international buying trips, far from her Cahokia home. Today she resides in Sun City, Arizona. (Courtesy Rita LePere Howell.)

This is the wedding photo of Robert "Pete" LePere and Melinda Berghoefer. Joseph and Marcella Quevreaux were the attendants at the ceremony. (Courtesy Rita LePere Howell.)

Jerome "Jerry" and Mary Lopinot were married in April 1951 and have resided in Cahokia since 1955. Jerry is Cahokia's renowned historian. Mary taught at Chartrand, Maplewood, Centerville, E. Morris, and Huffman Schools. (Courtesy John Reed.)

Oliver and Rosemary Carron are pictured here on their wedding day, May 3, 1941. Attendants were Violet Kunkel Nagel and William Wegman. The Carrons moved to Cahokia in January 1951. (Courtesy Dolores Seats.)

This wedding photo of Charles Burton Jackson and Margaret Josephine Whalen was taken May 20, 1950. The Jacksons moved to 7 Dolores Drive, City View Subdivision, in Cahokia on September 10, 1955. (Courtesy Cahokia Unit School District #187 teacher Steve Jackson.)

Anna Mae Minning and Gerald Helton were married on May 23, 1954. (Courtesy Cahokia Unit School District #187 teacher Steve Jackson.)

Ron and Peg Cobb were married on November 4, 1956, and reside in the community. Ron can trace his Cahokia ancestors back to the 1870s. (Courtesy LaVerne Levin Cobb.)

Four

OUR CHILDREN

Children are a gift from God and are the future of all communities.

Florence Jerome was born on December 22, 1901. (Courtesy John Reed.)

This photo of LaVerne Levin, born in 1918, was taken in Cahokia when she was five months old. (Courtesy LaVerne Levin Cobb.)

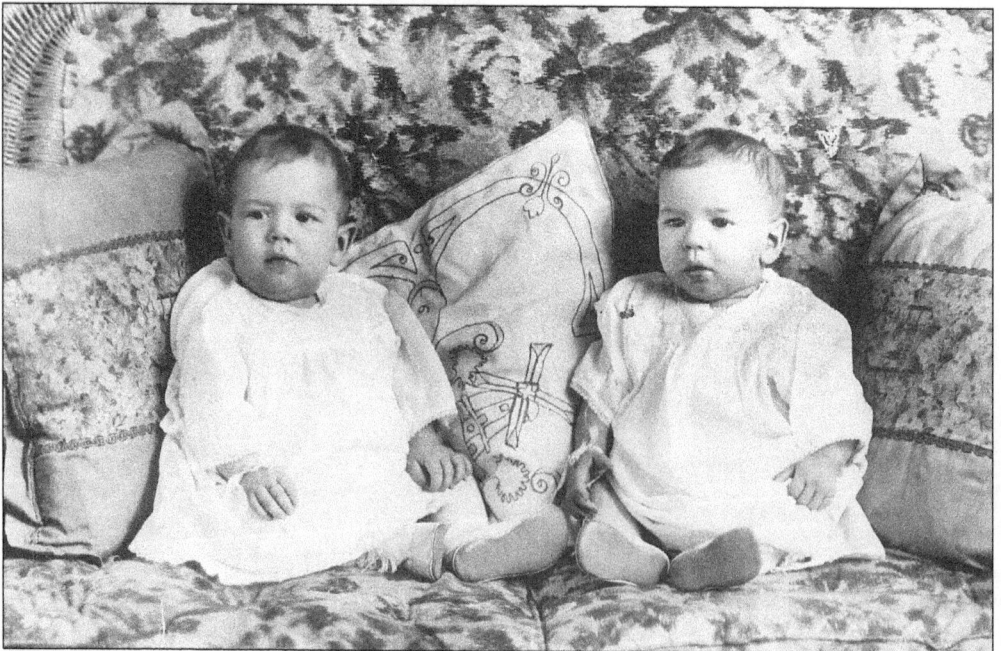

Twins Edgar and Edward Levin were born April 11, 1922, in Cahokia. (Courtesy LaVerne Levin Cobb.)

Albert Jerome was born on September 14, 1930. He was one year old when this photo was taken. Albert was ordained a priest on May 23, 1959. After various assignments, he returned to his home parish in 1977 as pastor and served at Holy Family until 1987. He currently is pastor at St. Ann Parish in Nashville, IL. (Courtesy Father Albert Jerome.)

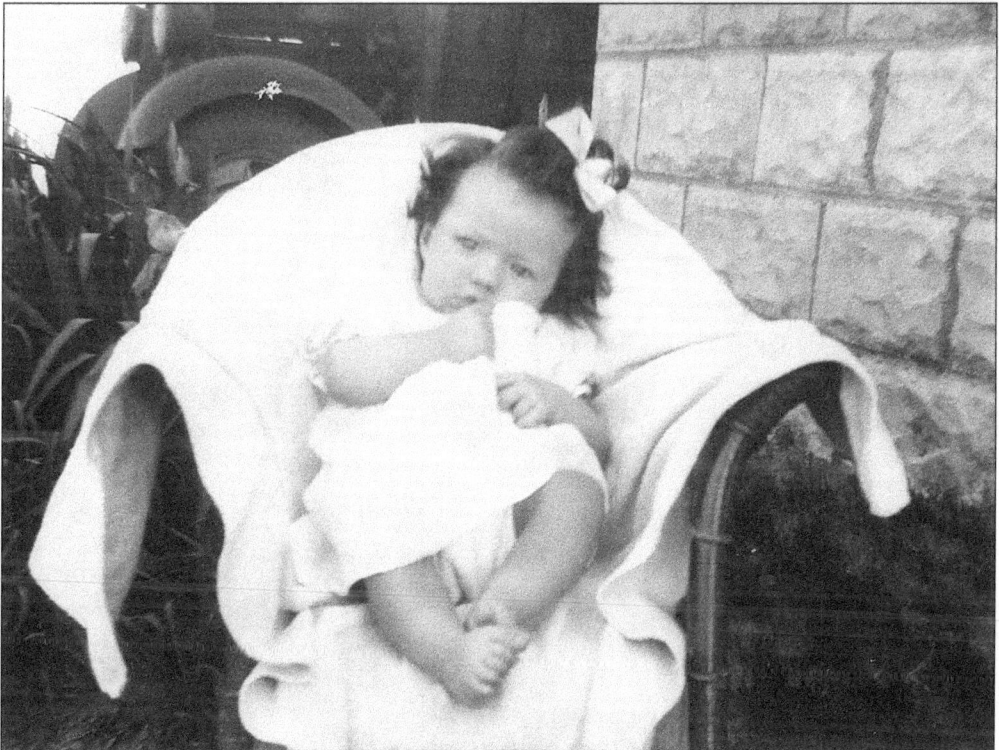

This snapshot of infant Ruth Emerson was taken at home on Levin Drive in Cahokia in 1944. (Courtesy Marilyn Emerson Holtzer.)

Little Linda Levin was almost two when this photo was taken on the porch of her family's "Village Stop." (Courtesy Family of Sonny and June Levin.)

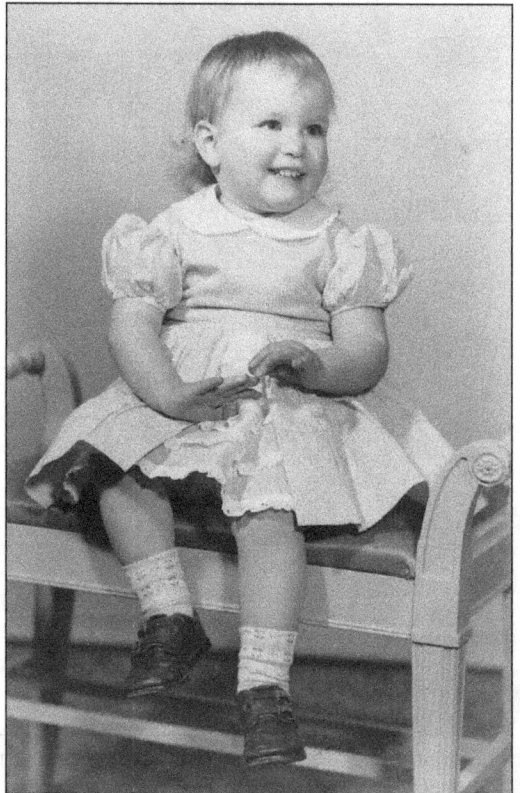

Loretta Lopinot, age two in this picture, grew up to be the library director of the Cahokia Public Library District, from 1977 to present. (Courtesy Lopinot Family.)

Francis LaValle was three years old in this picture, c. 1921. The family lived at the Abbey House when it was a private residence. The Abbey House was located on Cahokia Commons across from Holy Family Church. (Courtesy Rita LePere Howell.)

Jerome "Jerry" Lopinot traces his Cahokia ancestors to the 1800s. He is now a St. Clair County judge and is fondly known as Cahokia's chief historian. (Courtesy Lopinot Family.)

This photo was taken at the Levin family home, located at 2300 Jerome Lane, in 1923. Grandmother Mary Chattillion with Marie Moreano and twins Edward and Edgar Levin are pictured here. Grandson Elmer Levin, three years old, is pictured holding the handle of the cart. (Courtesy LaVerne Levin Cobb.)

Twins Edward and Edgar Levin are dressed in band uniforms for their Maplewood School Orchestra performance. (Courtesy LaVerne Levin Cobb.)

Albert Jerome looks quite handsome in his Maplewood School band uniform. (Courtesy Father Albert Jerome.)

Jerry Lopinot and a friend enjoy sitting cross-legged on the porch. (Courtesy Lopinot Family.)

Baby Albert Jerome with his sisters Mary Lou and Betty appear in this photo from 1931. (Courtesy Father Albert Jerome.)

Siblings Albert, Betty, and Mary Lou Jerome are pictured at the family home on Jerome Lane in the mid-1930s. (Courtesy Father Albert Jerome.)

Rita LePere's crepe-paper dress was
fashioned for a school play in 1931.
(Courtesy Rita LePere Howell.)

The LePere home on the corner of Plum and
Third Street is one of the oldest dwellings
in the community today. Pictured here are
Rosemary Muckerman and Rita LePere,
c. 1930. Rosemary currently resides in
St. Louis and belongs to the Sisters of Notre
Dame. Rita is retired and lives in Sun City,
Arizona. (Courtesy Rita LePere Howell.)

Little Marilyn Emerson poses in a zinnia flower garden at the Sauget farm on Plum Street. (Courtesy Marilyn Emerson Holtzer.)

Marjorie, Roberta, and Marilyn Emerson stand in front of their house on Levin Drive in Cahokia. Roberta is dressed in a flower girl dress for a wedding. All the dresses were made by their mother, Ethel Emerson, c. 1942–43. (Courtesy Marilyn Emerson Holtzer.)

Five

OUR FAMILIES

We celebrate the many families who have called Cahokia home throughout its 300 years.

This photo of the Boismenue family was taken at their home in Cahokia in the early 1900s. The elderly man seated in the middle has been identified as great-grandfather Nicholas Boismenue. Standing over his right shoulder is his son, Eli Ambrose Boismenue, with his hand on the shoulder of his wife, Amber. Amber holds baby Hazel in her lap. (Courtesy Joyce Wilkinson.)

Jerome family members gather in 1902 at Grandpa Jean Baptiste's barn on Jerome Lane. The goat in the foreground was a pet of Rose and Florence Jerome. The Jerome family came to Cahokia in 1830. In 1927, the *St. Louis Globe Democrat* reported, "there are more Jeromes than you can count on all your fingers and toes." There were 21 registered Jerome voters in Cahokia. (Courtesy John Reed.)

Grandfather Godin poses with his horse in Prairie du Pont, at the southern edge of Cahokia, c. 1830. (Courtesy LaVerne Levin Cobb.)

In this photo dated 1912, Jules and Armentine Levin are at work on the old family farm located in Cahokia, near the Prairie du Pont Canal Bridge. Jules was born in France in 1847, entered the United States in 1868, and married on June 3, 1871. (Courtesy LaVerne Levin Cobb.)

Leo Sauget and his friend Foster enjoy fishing at a Cahokia lake. (Courtesy Marguerite Mischke.)

Chatillion and Levin brothers pose for the camera in the early 1900s. (Courtesy LaVerne Levin Cobb.)

Grandma and Grandpa Sauget's 50th wedding anniversary party, c. 1918, was attended by many family members. They are, from left to right, as follows: (front row) Marguerite Sauget Mischke, Vincent Sauget, Alebartile Sauget, Louise Sliment Keck, Ellen Sliment Peterson, Estella Sauget Pillard, Emile Sauget, Leo Sliment, Ester Adele Gruenewald, Norman Stieb, Theophile Sauget, and Wallace Sauget; (second row) Irvin Sauget, Carl Sauget, Ernest Sauget, Armand Sauget, Pauline Sauget, Henrietta Stieb, Eugenia Adele, Norval Adele, Ida Sauget, and Arthur Sauget; (third row) Sylvester Sauget, Antoinette Sauget Taylor, Louise Adele Sauget, Maria Adele Sauget, Georgette Sauget, Henry Sauget, Mary Mueller, Louise Sauget Conroy, Della Soucy, Ida Sauget, Gertrude Soucy, Corrine Dickerson, and Joseph Adele; (back row) Arthur Stieb, James Sliment, Eugene Sauget, Elmer Soucy, Leo Sauget, William Mueller, Clarence Sauget, and Stephen Soucy. (Courtesy Georgette Sauget, Marguerite Mischke, and Richard Sauget.)

This photo of the Eugene Baptiste and Maria Augusta (Adele) Sauget family was taken at the family's farmhouse, c. 1918. (Courtesy Georgette Sauget.)

Lena, Nick, and August Adele are shown here at their farmhouse on the corner of Jerome and Range Lane. The property is now occupied by Cahokia High School. (Courtesy Homer Adele.)

Albert L. and Elizabeth (Pluff) Jerome (at center) pose for a family portrait with their children Camille, Oscar, Eshter, and Leo. (Courtesy Father Albert Jerome.)

Leo and Tillie Jerome are pictured here with the family car on Jerome Lane in 1939. (Courtesy Father Albert Jerome.)

Leon Pluff and Marion Lowry pose in front of Leon's parents' home at 750 Jerome Lane. The elder Pluffs, Fred and Clara, moved into this home on their wedding day in 1909. (Courtesy Leon and Marion Pluff.)

Cahokia resident Jerry Lopinot, shown here in his Navy uniform, poses with his sister Faye and his mother, Rose, while on leave from Davisville, Rhode Island, in July 1943. (Courtesy Lopinot Family.)

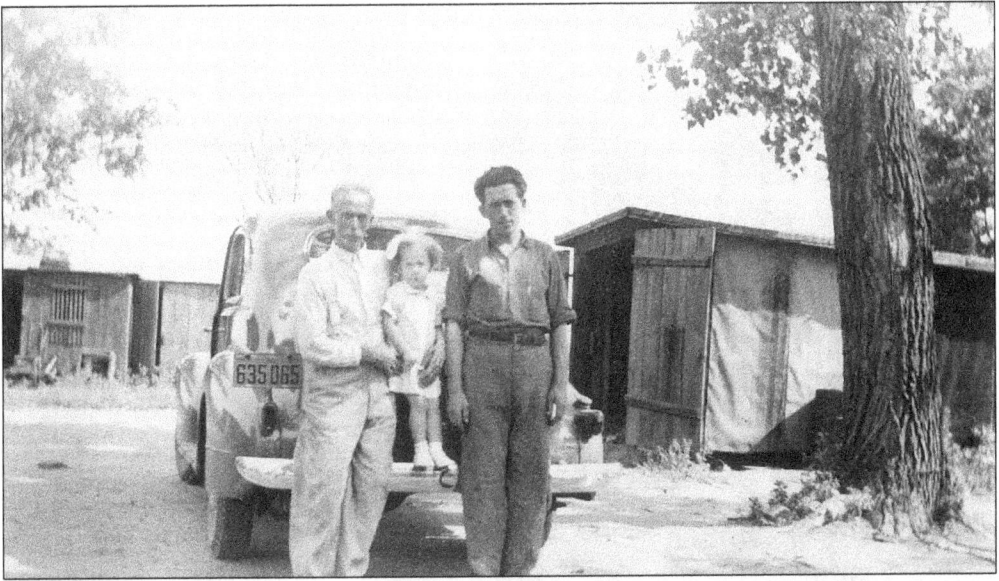

Phyllis Jerome, age four, is held by her grandfather, Charles Jerome Jr., at the family farm at Range and Doris. Phyllis's father, Earl Jerome, is on the right. (Courtesy Phyllis Jerome Taylor.)

Arthur LePere was the first mayor of Cahokia after the village was incorporated in 1927. He served from 1928 to 1943. The LePere family, including Robert "Pete," Arthur, Nelia, Petronella, and Rita, is pictured here. (Courtesy Rita LePere Howell.)

Rita LePere Howell, shown here with her children, two-year-old Nicoletta and five-year-old Gregory, has traced her LaValle ancestors in Cahokia to the 1770s. (Courtesy Rita LePere Howell.)

The Sauget family farm was one of the first in Illinois to be designated as a Centennial Farm by the Illinois Historical Society. Armand Sauget purchased the farm in 1870. The 50-acre tract is still farmed today by family members. Pictured in April 1959 are Grandma Sauget with grandchildren Jean, Marjorie, and Dan. (Courtesy Georgette Sauget.)

This portrait of Leo Sauget and Louise Julia (Adele) Sauget was made on the occasion of their 50th birthdays. Leo Sauget served as mayor of Monsanto from 1926 to 1969. The town was later named Sauget in his honor. (Courtesy Marguerite Mischke and Richard Sauget.)

This portrait of Clarence (Sonny) and June Levin was taken in honor of their 25th wedding anniversary. The couple ran Sonny's Village Stop in Cahokia and shared the love and respect of many friends and relatives in the community. (Courtesy Family of Sonny and June Levin.)

Memories of loved ones and community members are always present in Cahokia. Neighbors of June Levin planted a tree in a neighborhood "common field" after her death in 1997. Levin family members pose here for a picture by the living memorial. (Courtesy Denita Reed.)

Many native Cahokia sons served their civic duty in various wars throughout history. Jack Fultz, pictured here with sister Marilyn and his parents, Olivette and Cliff, served in the Korean War. (Courtesy Olivette Barbier Fultz.)

Olivette Fultz and her daughter, Marilyn Towler, pose with Fete Fracaise medals awarded to Olivette's father. The medals were presented to Mr. Barbier at Fetes held in Falling Springs in 1912 and 1914. (Courtesy Denita Reed.)

Vincent and Estelle Sauget returned to Vatan, France, to visit the area where their ancestors lived. Grandfather Armand Sauget was born in Vatan on May 5, 1843. Many area residents have visited France to see the country where their families once lived. (Courtesy Richard Sauget.)

Six

OUR COMMUNITY

The Cahokia community includes historic buildings, businesses, organizations, and many individuals who contribute to make the community a fine place to live, work, and conduct daily business.

This 1841 lithograph of old Cahokia, *Cahokia in Winter*, is credited to J.C. Wild. The Jarrot Mansion (the building with three chimneys) and Holy Family Log Church (with its steeple) appear in the center of the lithograph. (Courtesy Cahokia Courthouse State Historic Site.)

The Cahokia Courthouse, built by the Sauciers as a private home in 1740, has also been used as a courthouse, town hall, school, saloon, and farm storage shed. Re-enactors gather around the courthouse in this photo from the 1995 Fete du Bon Vieux Temps. (Courtesy Cahokia Unit School District #187 teacher Sue Henderson.)

Norma Rey, Irene Rey, and Grandma Rey pose with out-of-town guests on the Cahokia Courthouse logs as the building was waiting to be reassembled in 1936. A rededication of the courthouse was held on May 30, 1949. (Courtesy Montine Family.)

This modern postcard depicts the treasured Jarrot Mansion. Built for native Frenchman Nicholas Jarrot in 1810, the mansion has the distinction of being the oldest masonry building in the state of Illinois. (Courtesy James R. Buck.)

The Jarrot Mansion is pictured here c. 1894, complete with its high-style Victorian porch and steel roof. The carriage house/wash house is directly to left of the mansion. (Courtesy Cahokia Courthouse State Historic Site.)

This rear view of the Jarrot Mansion is believed to have been taken in 1934 through HABS (Historic American Buildings Survey). Note the kitchen ell addition on the right and the Spanish tile roof. (Courtesy Cahokia Courthouse State Historic Site.)

JARROT MANSION

This landmark structure has withstood time, owners, and many different uses. It remains remarkably intact today. The Jarrot Mansion was completed in 1810 for Nicholas Jarrot, a native Frenchman who achieved prosperity through trade, land, and law in frontier Cahokia. This building is the oldest brick house in Illinois.

An emphasis is placed on preserving the extensive original fabric of the Jarrot Mansion. Restoration is a solution when tested preservation measures fail.

"Old friends are worth keeping."

FOR MORE INFORMATION Cahokia Courthouse Historic Site Visitor Center
107 Elm Street, Cahokia · (618) 332-1782

The Illinois Historic Preservation Agency (IHPA) oversees the preservation measures of the Jarrot Mansion. The building is unique due to the extensive original materials. "Old friends are worth keeping." (Courtesy Cahokia Unit School District # 187 teacher Sue Henderson.)

Ms. Rose Josephine Boylan was instrumental in leading preservation efforts at all of the Cahokia sites. She is pictured here in the 1960s leading a tour for Cahokia High School students at the Jarrot Mansion. She is best remembered in the community for her knowledge of history and tireless efforts to preserve the heritage of Cahokia. (Courtesy Cahokia Unit School District #187 teacher Dale Goldsmith.)

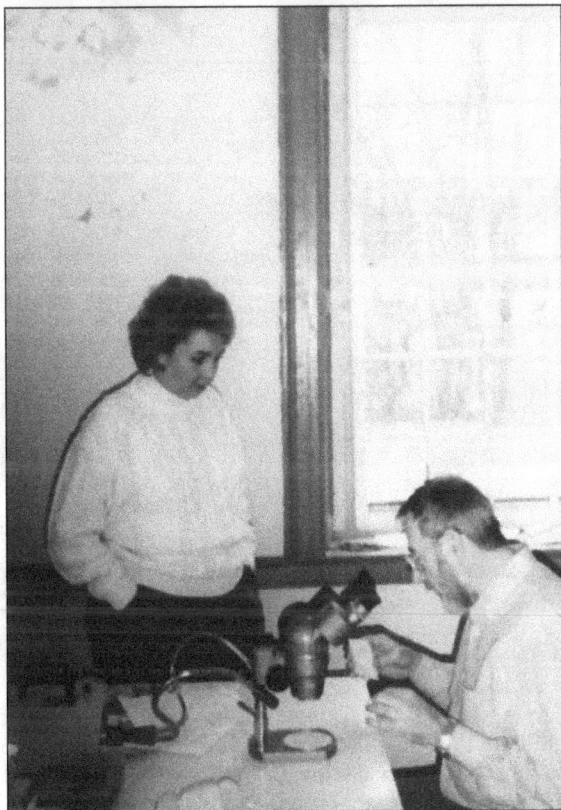

Pictured here are Ms. Molly McKenzie, site director of the Jarrot Mansion and Cahokia Courthouse State Historic Sites since 1981, and Robert Furhoff, paint analysis consultant. Through the efforts of Illinois Senator James Clayborne, $500,000 has been appropriated to preserve and open the mansion for Cahokia's tricentennial celebration. (Courtesy Denita Reed.)

Cahokia has had a history of destructive floods because of its proximity to the Mississippi River. This photo was taken during the flood of 1892. (Courtesy Holy Family Parish.)

These workers were employees of the St. Louis Cotton Compress Warehouse, which was built in 1902 to fill the needs of the growing St. Louis cotton shipping industry. Today the warehouse is managed by Sauget Properties, Ltd. and houses a variety of commercial trucking and warehousing tenants. (Courtesy Richard Sauget.)

The Hoock brothers proudly display their trapped animals from atop their automobile hood, c. 1910. (Courtesy Family of Chris Sutter and Lee Darnell.)

Cahokia hunters pose on the Stillman Farm, c. 1910. (Courtesy Family of Chris Sutter and Lee Darnell.)

This aerial view of the Holy Family Parish complex was taken in 1927. The rectory and Holy Family Rock Church are visible, although Holy Family Log Church is partially hidden by trees. The Abbey House is pictured in the foreground. (Courtesy LaVerne Levin Cobb.)

This "Abbey House" was constructed on the grounds of the original "Abbey" convent and school. The 1890–1920 Abbey House was a taproom and dance hall. (Courtesy LaVerne Levin Cobb.)

Godin's Tavern at the corner of Jerome Lane and Upper Cahokia Road was a popular gathering place for Cahokians. This picture is dated 1909. (Courtesy Family of Chris Sutter and Lee Darnell.)

The Waterloo-St. Louis streetcar, Conaloga Line, was the favorite mode of transportation from 1912 to 1936. Among those pictured here are conductor Bill Peters and Arthur LePere (third from the left). (Courtesy Rita LePere Howell.)

This historic postcard depicts the mode of travel for Cahokia's village doctors, Alexis Illinski and Robert McCracken. The doctors served the community with humanity and charity from 1849 to 1889. (Courtesy LaVerne Levin Cobb.)

The Prairie du Pont Canal Bridge is pictured here during construction. The site is located on the southern edge of Cahokia. (Courtesy LaVerne Levin Cobb.)

94

Court Cafe was located 100 feet west of Route 3 and was a favorite gathering place for village residents. (Courtesy LaVerne Levin Cobb.)

A group of local residents are pictured at the bar of the Court Cafe, a popular meeting place and restaurant owned by Marion Helfrich. (Courtesy Family of Sonny and June Levin.)

Gus Mallett operated this grocery store on Route 3 in the early 1900s. (Courtesy Rita LePere Howell.)

This photo of the Levin Tavern and Grocery store was taken in 1927. The building was owned by Alfred Levin, and members of both the Levin and Pulcher families are pictured in the foreground. (Courtesy Elmer Levin.)

Commercialism boomed in the region after 1920, with the growth of an industrial area between East St. Louis and Cahokia. The Monsanto Chemical Company, the Cahokia Power Plant of Union Electric, the Lillrite Refining Company, the Lewin Metals Corporation, the Midwest Rubber Reclaiming Company, and the Phillips 66 Petroleum Company all brought jobs and opportunities for the small community. Pictured here are Monsanto employees in the early 1940s. (Courtesy John Reed.)

These spectators at a Sunday morning trap meeting have been identified as wives and children of Monsanto employees. Sitting down are, from left to right, Mrs. Wells, Mrs. Sauget (wife of Monsanto Mayor), Mrs. Reed, and Mrs. Davis. (Courtesy John Reed.)

Cahokia-Maplewood
Volunteer Fire Department

WHAT TO DO IN CASE OF FIRE:

1. Keep calm; don't get excited. Don't delay; call at once. A call in time may save yours and mine (home or homes).

2. Call Hemlock 320.

3. Give the name and place of fire. Also number on bottom of this card.

4. Check call a minute or two later to see if Cahokia-Maplewood Fire Department has been contacted.

5. Be ready to assist the Firemen by removing any obstruction that may hinder operation of the equipment.

6. Check available water supply and make same ready for a bucket brigade. Fill all available containers.

DON'T DELAY! CALL . . .

-HEMLOCK 320-

The Cahokia-Maplewood Volunteer Fire Department's 1946 flyer outlined emergency instructions for residents. (Courtesy Cahokia Volunteer Fire Department.)

These Cahokia-Maplewood Volunteer Fire Department firemen from 1946 have been identified, from left to right, as follows: (kneeling) T. Sauget, C. Sauget, N. LaCroix, J. Alexander, H. Erndle, and T. Mooney; (standing) N. Viner, W. Lucher, K. Whittaker, C. White, H. Frick, F. Engler, unidentified, and C. Viner. (Courtesy Jerry Callahan and John Nowak.)

These Cahokia-Maplewood Community Fire Department members in 1954 have been identified, from left to right, as follows: (front row) Assistant Chief Francis Jerome, Chief Paul Bown, and Assistant Chief Ray Vernon; (second row) Herbie Talbott, John Marchand, Calvin Viner, Don Chaudet, Walter Maness, Charles Brewer, Tom Mooney, and Calvin Brewer; (third row) Charles Gill, C. Earl Jerome, Walter Crouch, Theophile Sauget, George Harmon, Jerome Wayne, Herman Erndle, and Donald Bacon; (back row) Kenneth Whittaker, Charles Sage, Ferd Engler, Orville Sackett, Herbert Walker, Phillip Rachell, James Lambert, Roy Hurt, Donald Duckworth, Herman Frick, John Wayne, and Clarence Sauget. (Courtesy Cahokia Volunteer Fire Department.)

C. Earl Jerome, president of the Cahokia-Maplewood Community Fire Department, made his farewell speech on fire protection at the Cahokia Fire House. (Courtesy Phyllis Jerome Taylor.)

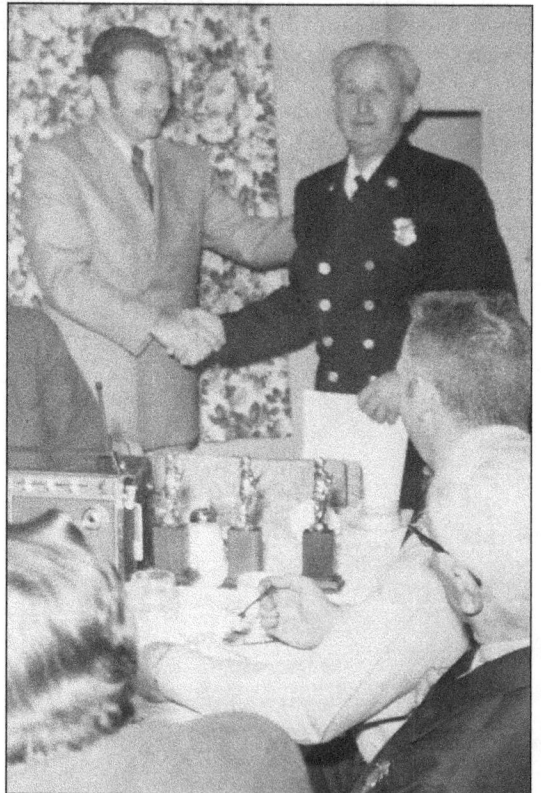

Cahokia Mayor Robert Jackson commends Cahokia Volunteer Fire Department Chief Herman Erndle for his years of service. (Courtesy Cahokia Volunteer Fire Department.)

Cahokia VFW Chief Pontiac Post 1699 performs color guard duties at Cahokia's 250th anniversary in 1949. (Courtesy Holy Family Parish and LaBusier Photography.)

The original home of VFW Chief Pontiac Post 1699 was on Upper Cahokia Road from 1940 to 1973. The VFW and its Ladies Auxiliary exemplify a long history of service to the Cahokia community. (Courtesy Cahokia VFW, Chief Pontiac Post 1699.)

The Cahokia VFW Chief Pontiac Post 1699 Past Commander Recognition ceremony was held in January 1983. From left to right are James Foutch, Pete LePere, John Hudson, Warren Weaver, Calvin Harwell, John Kloepple, Robert Nordike, and Eugene Redd. (Courtesy Cahokia VFW Chief Pontiac Post 1699.)

The Phillips Home Bureau was founded in October of 1953 by the wives of the men employed at the Phillips 66 Petroleum Company. This group picture was taken in May 1954 at the Phillips Community House. (Courtesy Marilyn Fultz Towler.)

Charter member Mrs. Olivette Fultz was the publicity chair and chief historian for the Phillips Home Bureau. In October 1957, the group opened membership to all ladies of the community and became known as "Cahokia Homemakers." (Courtesy Olivette Barbier Fultz.)

The Cahokia Squaws service organization was formed in 1954. Civic projects included art shows, rummage sales, charity drives, carnivals, aid to the needy, and beautification of historic landmarks. (Courtesy Jean LaForge Chiasson.)

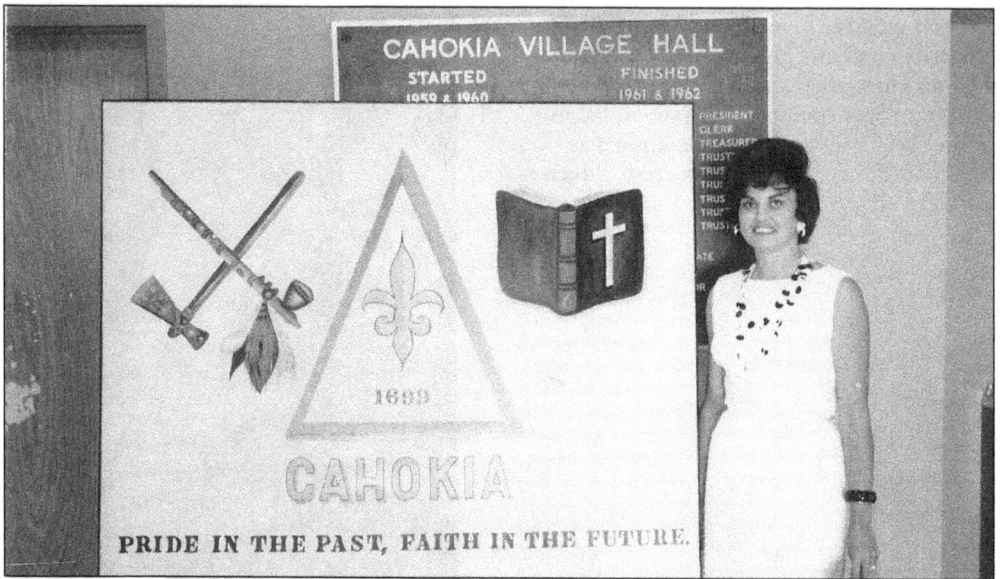

Jean LaForge, Cahokia Squaws president from 1962 to 1963, is pictured here with the winning design in the Squaws-sponsored Cahokia Flag & Motto Contest. Carla Pluff designed the flag, which continues to be used today. (Courtesy Jean LaForge Chiasson.)

The Cahokia Garden Club has been in existence since March 1958. Through the years, the club has contributed much beauty to the village with community flower beds and plantings, Arbor Day programs for schoolchildren, and floral displays for the Cahokia Library. In this photo, Cahokia Garden Club members are shown tending their circular garden at the Blue Star Memorial Highway marker in the spring of 1974. (Courtesy Mary Ellen Lindsey.)

Parade participants gather at Sutter's Mobilgas Service Station at the corner of Route 3 and First Street. (Courtesy Family of Sonny and June Levin.)

Flinn's Market opened in Cahokia in September 1953 on Highway 157, near the eastern border of Cahokia. Cahokia resident Monroe Flinn served as Illinois State Representative from Cahokia from 1971 to 1995. He was most proud of his new 1955 Ford (far right). (Courtesy State Representative Monroe Flinn, retired.)

After World War II, Oliver Parks responded to the need for low-cost housing for young couples by developing subdivisions of prefabricated homes. In this photo, a resident enters a home in St. Joseph's Gardens, the first of these subdivisions. City View, Bridgedale, Parklane Manor, St. Louis Gardens, and St. John's soon followed. (Courtesy Holy Family Parish.)

Maplewood Tom Boy's grand opening was held in 1955. The store, owned by Dave Kramer, was located at the corner of Upper Cahokia Road and Chaudet. (Courtesy Holy Family Parish.)

St. John Drive in Parklane Manor is pictured in this photo taken during the flood of 1957. (Courtesy Eleanor Schuh.)

Local television personality Texas Bruce was a hit with area children when Kenny's Shoe Store featured the celebrity in the late 1950s. (Courtesy Jean LaForge Chiasson.)

Centreville Township Hospital was formed in 1958 by Francis Touchette to provide for the needs of the community. The hospital was later renamed Touchette Regional Hospital in honor of its founder. (Courtesy Touchette Regional Hospital and Laureen Lawson.)

Francis Touchette was legendary in his commitment to quality healthcare for community members. The hospital remains dedicated to providing care for everyone regardless of their ability to pay. (Courtesy Touchette Regional Hospital and Laureen Lawson.)

Cahokia developer Kenneth LaForge and Mr. Wolff show the plans for the Cahokia Village Shopping Center to Mr. Joe Livigni in this photo dated July 15, 1971. (Courtesy Jean LaForge Chiasson.)

Residents are quite proud of Cahokia Park, which features the village swimming pool, ice rink, and The Prairies Golf Course. The Cahokia Public Library District and Senior Citizen's Center are also located in the park. The current mayor is Michael King. (Courtesy Cahokia Unit School District #187 teacher Sue Henderson.)

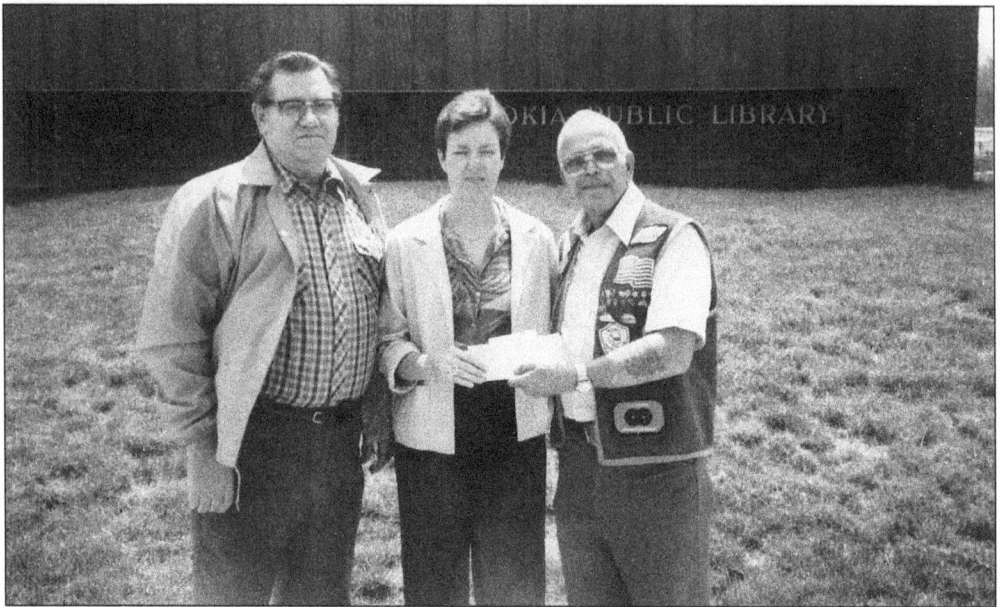

John Woodside of the American Legion Post 784 Honor Guard and Frank Maloney of the Cahokia Jaycees presented a donation to Library Director Loretta Lopinot. Started in 1962 in a garage, the Cahokia Public Library occupied space in both the village hall and a storefront. The construction of a library building in 1982 was realized through the visionary efforts of library trustees and the generosity of local residents, organizations, and businesses. (Courtesy Cahokia Public Library District.)

Cahokia's first recorded population of 30 white fur traders in 1700 has now grown to 18,900, as recorded on this current village sign. The actual 1990 census counts 17,550 as the population figure, with the next census scheduled to be conducted in the year 2000. (Courtesy Cahokia Unit School District #187 teacher Sue Henderson.)

Seven

OUR CELEBRATIONS

The people's celebrations in the Cahokia community have been as simple as picnics and birthday parties, and as elaborate as Pontifical Masses and grand pageants. Each celebration, no matter how large or small, unites and strengthens the people and the community.

This photo depicts a musical gathering at Charles "Red Charlie" Jerome's home in Cahokia, c. 1890. (Courtesy Mae Jerome Wayne and Cahokia Courthouse State Historic Site.)

Shown here posing in a c. 1895 Falling Springs photograph are Gus Schwarzstrauber, Arthur LePere, unidentified, and Walter LePere. (Courtesy Rita LePere Howell.)

Mary (Marie) Morineau Sutter was photographed at Falling Springs in 1910. Located south of the village of Cahokia, Falling Springs was a popular picnic site for generations. Visitors came from near and far to enjoy the picturesque setting. (Courtesy Family of Chris Sutter and Lee Darnell.)

In the fall, chicken suppers on the Holy Family Log Church lawn would bring locals, as well as residents from neighboring communities, together on Sundays. (Courtesy Cahokia Courthouse State Historic Site and Mike Dunn.)

Ethel Emerson poses with her daughter Marilyn and friends at Marilyn's birthday party in July 1942. (Courtesy Marilyn Emerson Holtzer.)

This 1942 celebration featured Cahokians as queen and court members. Participants have been identified as Queen Armida Sutter, Louise Levin, JoAnn Hill, Betty Woods, and Helen Demetrulias. The gentlemen in 18th-century costume were from the county historical society. (Courtesy Betty Woods Leilich.)

State and church officials and Fourth Degree Knights of Columbus members gathered at a ceremony on the Log Church lawn. Holy Family Rock Church is visible in the left of the photo; the clapboard-covered Log Church is shown at right. (Courtesy Holy Family Parish.)

Many special occasions of Holy Family Parish were marked by luncheon and dinner gatherings held in the Holy Family Primary School cafeteria. (Courtesy Holy Family Parish.)

Alice Viner (Soucy) and Clarence "Butch" Touchette celebrate New Year's Eve at the Viner family home in 1949. (Courtesy Rita LePere Howell.)

Village residents were photographed at the Cahokia Courthouse in preparation for Cahokia's 250th anniversary celebration in 1949. The residents shown here are, from left to right, as follows: (front row) Walter Lucher, Maurice Holley, Wally Sauget, Leo Jerome, and Ralph Leigh; (middle row) Louis Rey, Bob Jerome, Eugene Burns, Sonny Levin, and Dutch Timer; (back row) Pete Montine, Richard Haskenhoff, Ernie Sauget, and Ken Whittaker. (Courtesy Norman A. Viner.)

Bishop Joseph Schlarmann and dignitaries enter Holy Family Rock church for a 1949 Celebration Mass. (Courtesy Holy Family Parish.)

The opening ceremony for the 250th anniversary celebration was held May 14, 1949. The event took place on what was once the common-held land of the settlers of the French village of Cahokia. Most of the hierarchy of the Catholic Church in Illinois attended the event. (Courtesy Cahokia Courthouse State Historic Site.)

A solemn Pontifical Mass was celebrated on this outdoor altar with more than 10,000 guests in attendance. (Courtesy Holy Family Parish and LaBusier Photography.)

A dramatization of the village's founding in 1699 was performed during the 250th anniversary celebration. The Reverend Joseph P. Donnelly, S.J., Ph.D., Adolph B. Seuss, and Rose Josephine Boylan served on the Pageant Script Committee. (Courtesy Holy Family Parish.)

This birthday party celebration in 1954 was held in Harvest Acres subdivision. The children in the front row have been identified as Judy Bryer, John Reed, Joe Morice, and Danny Erndle. (Courtesy John Reed.)

Local TV personalities Cooky and The Captain made a guest appearance at the Holy Family School picnic in 1960. Mary Schuh is the little girl with the Captain. (Courtesy Eleanor Schuh.)

In 1963, the Cahokia Junior Woman's Club revived the custom of La Gui-annee, a French Canadian celebration, with a gala ball. Mrs. Kenneth (Jean) LaForge was the 1965 LaGui-annee queen. (Courtesy Jean LaForge Chiasson.)

La Gui-annee singers performed at the La Gui-annee Ball, January 19, 1974. The singers are, from left to right, Norman Viner, Dave Touchette, Pete LePere, Kenneth LaForge, Elias "Ducker" Chiasson, Jerry Lopinot, Leo Jerome, Vincent Lopinot, and Virgil "Smoky" Pluff. (Courtesy Jean LaForge Chiasson.)

The 25th anniversary celebration of the revived custom of La Gui-annee was held January 21, 1989. Many attendees dressed in period costume to celebrate the rich heritage of the Cahokia community. Milice de Ste. Famille member Bill Wheeler and his wife, Ann, are pictured near the stage. (Courtesy Denita Reed.)

Lisa Schilling and Lorie Crites participate in a 13-Star Day parade. These celebrations were held to commemorate George Rogers Clark's visit to Cahokia in 1778 and the allegiance of Cahokians to the American Revolutionary cause. (Courtesy Eleanor Schuh.)

Knights of Columbus Cahokia Council #4596 participate in the 1976 13-Star Day celebration with this float. (Courtesy Guy Baney.)

Cahokia residents Guy R. Baney and Frank Braun stand before the Braun Colonial Funeral Home antique hearse during the Cahokia Homecoming parade of 1983. (Courtesy Guy Baney.)

An alumni reunion was held on September 15, 1990, at the Jarrot Mansion. The mansion was used as a school from 1905 to 1941. (Courtesy Cahokia Courthouse State Historic Site.)

Re-enactors portray the colonial militia, Milice de Ste. Famille, at Frog Talk in 1990. (Courtesy Cahokia Courthouse State Historic Site.)

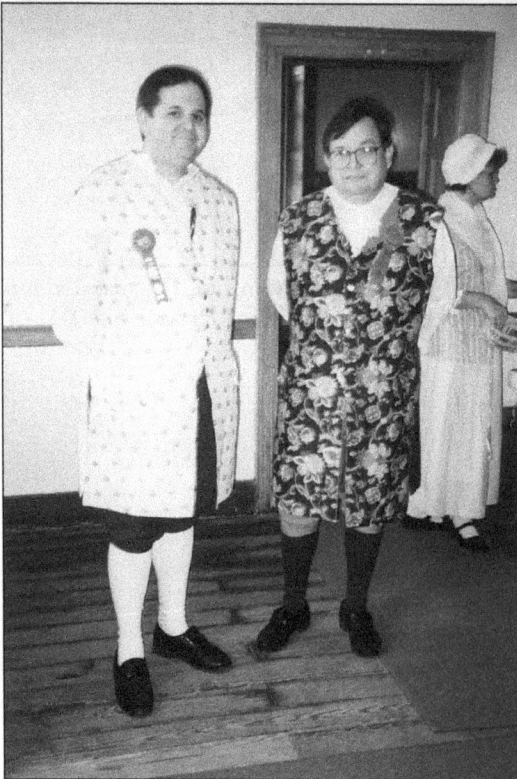

Jarrot Mansion project volunteers included Illinois State Representative Tom Holbrook and Attorney Russell Scott acting as tour guides at the Jarrot Mansion during the 1995 Fete du Bon Vieux Temps. (Courtesy Cahokia Unit School District # 187 teacher Sue Henderson.)

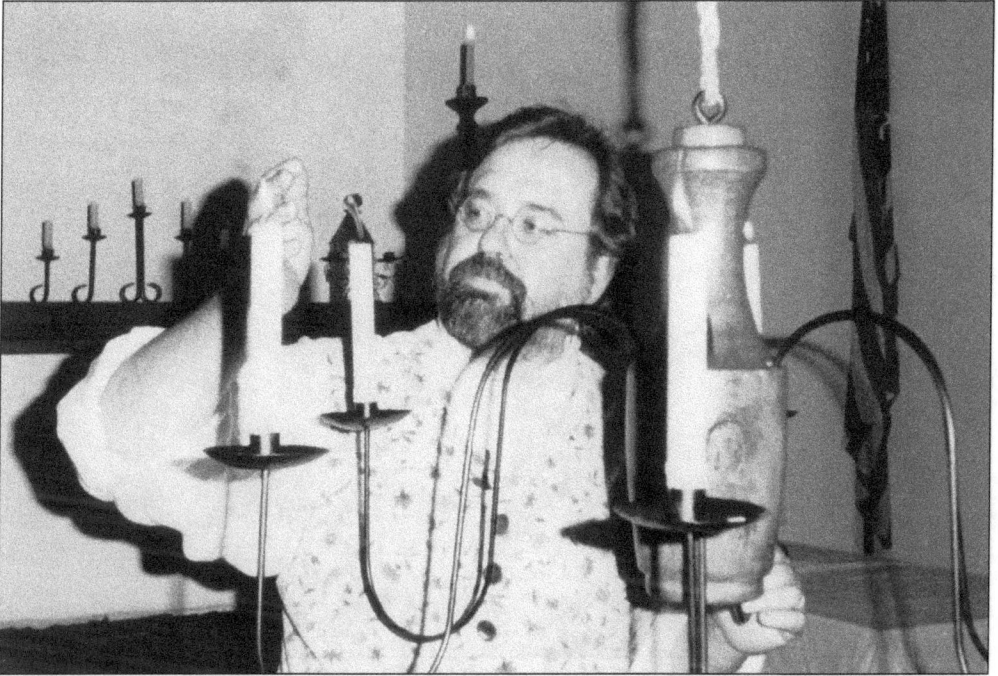

Cahokia Courthouse volunteer, Fete committee member, and blacksmith Ken Valdejo lights a candelabra that he hand-forged for the Cahokia Courthouse. (Courtesy Denita Reed.)

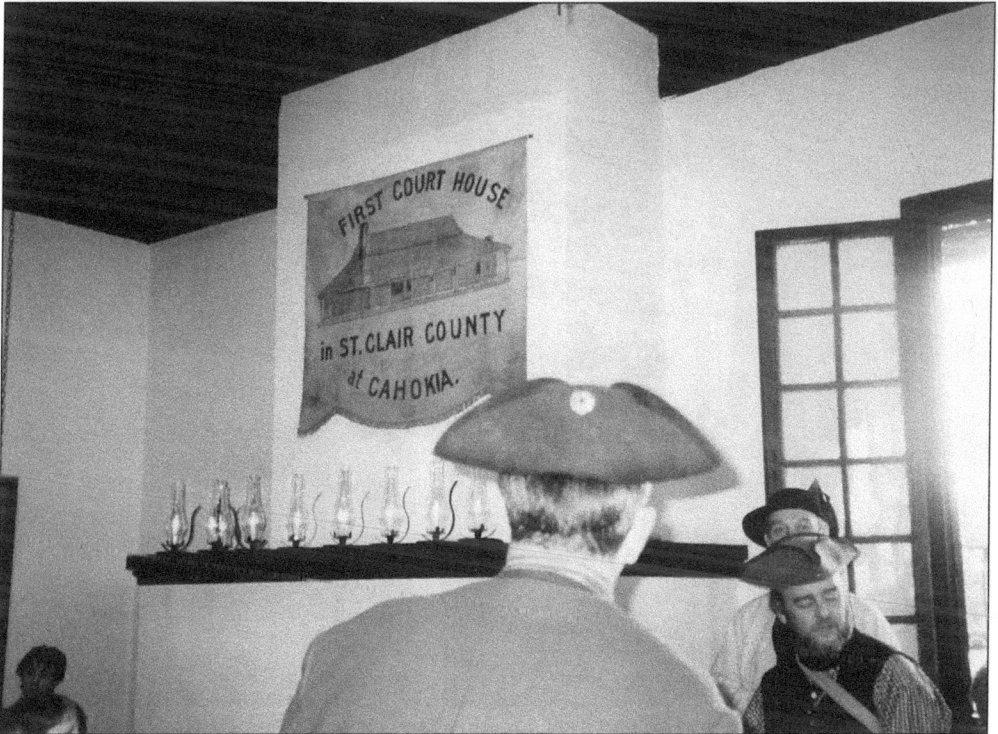

The interior of the Cahokia Courthouse is shown here during the 1995 Fete du Bon Vieux Temps. (Courtesy Cahokia Unit School District # 187 teacher Sue Henderson.)

Floyd Mansberger (right), owner of Fever River Research, conducts an archaeological dig at the Jarrot Mansion in 1993. He is assisted by Illinois State Representative Tom Holbrook. (Courtesy Denita Reed.)

The 1993 Holy Family Parish Rendezvous featured an encampment by the Milice de Ste. Famille. Those who walked through the camp were treated to a living history lesson. (Courtesy Denita Reed.)

Cahokia resident Mae Jerome Wayne, 93 years old, was the guest of honor at the 1992 Old Time Porch Music Fete. Her family photo was used to publicize the event. (Courtesy Denita Reed.)

Musicians perform in a "Super Jam" finale at the Old Time Porch Music Fete, held at the Cahokia Courthouse. (Courtesy Denita Reed.)

Connie Rutledge, LaVerne Cobb, and Bertha Taylor were all first-time participants at the Cahokia Public Library District's Christmas cookie exchange. The event will celebrate its 20th anniversary in December 1999. (Courtesy Denita Reed.)

Lifelong Cahokia residents Denita and John Reed were blessed to attend a mass in Pope John Paul II's private chapel on April 1, 1993. Mother Teresa was also in attendance. The entire Cahokia community is preparing for a possible visit from Pope John Paul II during the tricentennial celebration year of 1999. The Pope is scheduled to visit St. Louis on January 26, 1999. (Courtesy Denita Reed.)